GET YOUR MOJO BACK

BECOME THE DIRECTOR OF YOUR LIFE
A HANDBOOK FOR DEPRESSION RECOVERY

BY ANTHONY POLANCO

GodXP Publishing

FROM DEPRESSION TO
TRUE SELF-CONFIDENCE.

HOW-TO DEVELOP YOUR MASTER MIND
THE MOMENTUM EQUATION
DISCOVER YOUR EXISTENTIAL IDENTITY
MISJUDGMENT, PRESENTNESS, SELF-RELIANCE,+

GET MOJO

YOUR BACK

CLARIFY YOUR SELF-IMAGE
IMPROVE YOUR SOCIAL DYNAMICS
OVERCOME FEAR OF DEATH
CURE FOR DISAPPOINTMENT, +MORE
REVISED EDITION!

THE DEPRESSION RECOVERY FIELD MANUAL
BECOME THE DIRECTOR OF YOUR LIFE

ANTHONY POLANCO

TABLE OF CONTENTS

INTRODUCTION

"There is a time in every man's education when he arrives at the conviction that envy is ignorance; that imitation is suicide; that he must take himself for better, for worse, as his portion; that though the wide universe is full of good, no kernel of nourishing corn can come to him but through his toil bestowed on that plot of ground which is given to him to till. The power which resides in him is new in nature, and none but he knows what that is which he can do, nor does he know until he has tried."
— *Ralph Waldo Emerson, Self-Reliance*

My Story

It was my first year of college, a week before winter vacation.

I was driving my parents' GMC Yukon at about 70 miles per hour down a lone highway in the middle of the day. I must've blacked out. I opened my eyes and saw a Ford F-150 truck directly in front of me.

I jerked the wheel with all my might to the right, but it was too late. Our two vehicles clipped noses sending mine rolling across the highway. I don't remember the impact.

I only remember three scenes in glimpses from right before the moment to the hospital bed two hours later. They can only be described as an out-of-body, light at the end of the tunnel-experience.

Even 10 years later, I'm still pretty sure I died and left my body. I was lifted into complete nothingness and saw the road. There were three ghostlike spirits standing over my dead body. Then I "came back."

I have a few flashes of consciousness, eyes closed and in absolute pain from the ambulance, to the MRI machine, to the hospital bed a few hours later.

It was exactly like in a movie. I guess that's how anyone would feel about watching themself die.

The nurse came in to see if I could move my limbs yet. I miraculously didn't break any bones, but since I couldn't move my limbs we'd wait and see the extent of the damage. It took about an hour to get my legs to respond. She brought me a phone and asked if there was anyone I could call.

I was so severely concussed I couldn't remember names, let alone phone numbers. My cell phone was either still in the car or smashed on the road somewhere. I knew my name was Anthony.

I sat staring at the phone for a few minutes. The moment the nurse walked back in; I remembered my childhood best friend Jacob's family house phone number.

As I started dialing it, the pattern to my dad's cell phone number revealed itself to me, so I phoned him instead. So, my parents were on their way.

In walks Sheriff.

He asks how it happened and if I was under the influence of marijuana. He pulled out my skateboard repair tool and asked me to explain why I had a weed pipe in the car. I showed him how it was a wrench and said "I was on the way to pick up my mom from work, and I woke up in the hospital."

Then he asked me a fateful question: "Where are the other two people who were in the car with you?" I was like: "There was no one else with me. Just me."

Sherriff: "The witnesses said there were two other people in the car with you."

Me: "Well they must've been angels watching out for me. I was alone in that car."

Sherriff: "Must have been."

Exit Sherriff.

It took me years to realize the connection between my out-of-body experience and what the Sheriff said. Seeing two spirits on the road over my dead body.

It's worth noting my driver side door was completely punched-in meaning there was no way for me to get myself out of the car. The sheriff insisted someone must've been there to pull me out because when the ambulance arrived, they found me laying on the side of the road with no explanation.

Make of that what you will.

I was seven days away from a trip to South Korea with my buddy.

Christian ministry was our plan - My only interest beside music.

When I was 11, my parents let me go to Kenya, Africa with a small ministry team and no family for a month. That should explain it well enough.

And 7 days from my crash I was in Seoul, South Korea with a walking cane.

I was in miserable leg pain the whole time.

I was also suffering a new brain fog, which I couldn't figure out. It was like I was all of a sudden experiencing life through an invisible window. I could see you, you could see me, but there was something off. I just didn't feel like myself anymore. I was unsure of everything.

It felt like my ability to communicate with God was severed by the concussion. Otherwise, it must've been a delusion all along. Either option puts a 19-year-old Christian missionary in a really bad spot, existentially speaking.

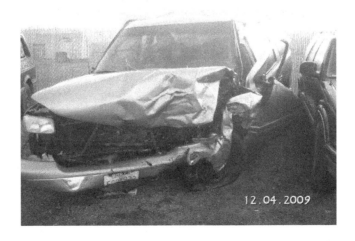

12.04.2009

How I Lost My Mojo

My life kept moving as if there was nothing wrong with me. As in no one seemed to recognize a difference. But the existential issues in my mind were increasing. My doubt in God increased because I no longer felt the same ways. I no longer believed myself. People around me seemed none the wiser.

My feelings and my thoughts weren't synchronizing like they used to. The after effects of my concussion were feeding the existential crisis. Over the next four years I unconsciously self-sabotaged everything good in my life.

My ego got away from me. I was seeing the world through a lot of delusion and false confidence. My band broke up, no one reached out. My girlfriend at the time finally had enough too. I'd already given up my early hairstyling career for a night janitor job and was living alone in a house on the outskirts of town. I finally had nothing. It took 4 years for my mental hell to fully reflect on the outside. Once the outside matched the inside, suicide seemed like the natural next step.

Staying on my parents' couch for a few days when I hit rock bottom, I finally admitted to myself that it was going to happen. In that moment I decided to tell my mom I was contemplating suicide. "If I don't get help in the next few days, I'm not going to make it." She made a Monday appointment with a therapist for me.

Later that day I was watching a post-practice interview of Kobe Bryant on YouTube and he mentioned a book by author Og Mandino.

I Googled and found his bestselling book from 1968 *The Greatest Salesman in The World*
I hadn't read a book since Freshman year of high school but Kobe was my hero. I had to give it a chance. I found a used copy for 5 dollars on eBay.

My Clinical Therapy Experience

I never felt free to express my existential problems to anyone before my first therapy appointment. I felt like people would think I was crazy or wouldn't understand my paradigm since it was so interwoven with my relationship to God. Therapy allowed me to express my confusion without feeling judged. He never told me what to think, or even how to think. He just gave me permission to express myself, so my subconscious dilemmas could come to light.

Within a month, my therapist retired.

Driving home from our final appointment, I was t-boned through an intersection on a green light, totaling my second car. God's got a strange sense of humor.

I decided not to replace my therapist.

How I Got My Mojo Back

Instead of replacing my therapist, I decided to start driving to the coast on the weekends to sing and play guitar for money. What did I have to lose? I was 24 with two friends and no job. I was reading three times a day listening to audiobooks on the road.

My Second Therapist

While playing in Monterey, CA one day two ladies stopped to listen and chat. One was in a wheelchair, and she was teaching yoga as therapy for MS patients. After hearing about my car accident, depression, and spiritual experience, she suggested I check out a way of meditating called kundalini yoga.

When I got home, I picked a YouTube video and sat on my bedroom floor. The 11-minute meditation video consisted mostly of vigorous breathwork exercise while holding my arms out to the sides, followed by a few minutes of silent meditation at the end.

Pranayama, breathing exercises and meditation are technology that bring you into extreme awareness of all that exists inside and beyond physical boundaries. Vigorous breathing exercises hyperoxygenate your blood, expanding your blood vessels, sending fresher blood to your brain, effectively giving you a temporary "superconsciousness." It is a mind-body technology that gives you spiritual strength. It immediately became my everyday practice.

Pranayama exercises are used across many yoga-meditation disciplines. Pranayama an ancient physiological science commonly referred to as yogic breathing. It is relative to any other form of breathing practice, in that the goal is to voluntarily build-up and relieve carbon dioxide with a resonant breathing pattern in order to enjoy the many positive benefits of hyperoxygenation. It is a matter of exercising the breath and consciously becoming its benefactor. It is a habit of using the breath to align the body and enter a primed state for optimal performance. It is the closest thing to having a real-life superpower that I've found.

And just like that, meditation became my second therapist through kundalini yoga. Kundalini yoga incorporates traditional asanas with pranayama, chanting, and meditation.

It is so helpful for people with depression because it forces you into awareness of your physical, mental, and spiritual self. The hyperoxygenation boosts mood and energy levels. Even just a 3-minute meditation can give you an intense euphoric feeling similar to being high on cannabis. I trip out on my own hyperoxygenated blood every night before bed and first thing every morning. Meditation with pranayama is the ultimate training center for your psychological and spiritual strength. That "superconscious" state is the optimal environment to pray and commune with God.

Discovering Knowledge

It took almost killing myself to actually understand the Thomas Jefferson adage "knowledge is power."

After reading Og Mandino's book that Kobe recommended to me through YouTube I realized that reading books about changing your life, surprisingly, will change your life if you let it.

Each subsequent book I read gave me even more self-understanding. I began asking myself better questions. I treated each book like the author was my mentor who wrote the book specifically for me.

I didn't want to waste time reading chaff, or hit books of the day that will be discarded by the next generation. I decided to start by reading the "all-time greats": Human achievers, philosophers, and leaders. As Sir Isaac Newton said, "If I have seen further, it is by standing upon the shoulders of giants."

From the great self-help writers like Emerson, Carnegie, and William Walker Atkinson, to classic philosophers like Seneca, Lao Tzu, and Socrates. I also became obsessed with reading biographies from many great achievers of all-time, and also time-tested behavioral psychology, business, and sales books. I was buying books on credit cards and reading them like they were water and I'd been in a desert dying of thirst.

In 2015 my friend Justin got me a gig running his bar's social media accounts. As soon as I landed a few more deals doing online copywriting and social media marketing, I quit my night janitor job and committed to starting my own digital marketing business.

My Third Therapist

My third therapist was a psychedelic experience with psilocybin mushrooms. I became drawn to psychedelics during my suicide ideation period. I listened to an audio lecture of Terrence Mckenna explaining the nature of psychedelic experimentation and its practical applications in the pursuit of lifelong consciousness expansion, or enlightenment.

It wasn't long before the Universe presented me with a heroic dose of psilocybin mushrooms to take alone in my bedroom. I prayed and fasted for 3 days. I asked God for forgiveness and grace.

At around 5pm I took four grams of psilocybin mushrooms along with about 3x too much THC-candy edibles, and for good measure began puffing on a hand-rolled cannabis flower cigarette. There I sat alone in my bedroom, in my empty house on the outskirts of town with a lamp, some incense burning, a notepad and a pencil.

In an hour, I was in ecstasy. In two hours, I no longer existed as far as I was concerned. My identity melted away. I died and became a witness to Infinity. What does infinity look like? Sound like? Feel like?

I weaved in and out of being every pattern, color, and sound through spacetime and beyond. A billion of each organic and energy form, and even more, because each and every unit of energy and matter has its own memories. There is a record of each form of matter that occupies space through time, and so there is a memory for it. The Universe by definition has infinite storage space. Within spacetime, only one thread of time can be observed at a time. Beyond spacetime, everything can be observed without limitations. God's perspective is beyond spacetime, God isn't bound my time, God's is the quantum perspective. By taking your consciousness out of spacetime, you can see from God's perspective. The quantum reality.

It lasted 10-12 hours by the clock, but it felt like I died. I got to witness life beyond the confines of "human." I saw my true identity as one of God's molecules. I saw that beyond the physical realm we are all simply burning light units, moving through God's body in spacetime, and to us it plays out like a human lifetime. The Name Above All Names. The Great I AM. The Source. Universal Intelligence. The framework of the Universe.

I was humbled with "God-realization." I became grateful for life itself like a prisoner reprieved from death. I felt my Oneness with the Universe. I felt my cosmic importance as an equal part of the eternal whole. It was better than that. It was deeper and more complex than I can explain without full use of expression, and even then, you just had to be there. And for all the cosmic spectacle and divine intimacy, my revelations were simple, as revelations tend to be. I was given a newfound love for life. I became self-aware, I felt "born again," and I realized every decision I make is a choice I make.

It is my responsibility to state regarding the use of psychedelics that I am not a medical expert, nor can I encourage the unsupervised use of psychedelics under any circumstance. If you are not prepared to go through complete and utter hell and never come back, don't do it. There are many brilliant scientific minds studying the use of psychedelics for mental health and I consider them the real heroes for psychedelic research and psychiatric applications. I am their cheerleader, an armchair philosopher. Outcomes with psychedelic experimentation are personal and unique and can be extreme. There is a cosmic price to pay for force-feeding yourself enlightenment. I have an obligation to speak my truth. You have the obligation to derive your own from it.

Starting A Business

With no friends, no life, no job, and nothing but perspective I figured I'd use it to my advantage and start something from scratch.

I invested all my money and free time in personal education - Digital marketing and consulting courses, coaching, conferences, networking events, business and personal development programs, and more books than I could read at once. I made big improvements in my health and my business, but still noticed my self-doubt and social struggles. I was still getting nervous on sales calls, and talking to girls, and I had no social life. So I turned to martial arts and signed up for Brazilian jiu-jitsu.

Growing my digital marketing client base while learning Brazilian jiu-jitsu, studying personal development, and meditating every day gave me competence at challenging things, which consistently built my self-confidence. Competence builds confidence.

Competence is a crucial factor in my feeling happier, and getting better and bigger. Competence has allowed me to pursue bigger goals, get out of debt, and to believe in myself to achieve even greater things than these. I chose these things because they relate to my personality and appeal to my nature. If you're unhappy with your life outcomes, maybe it's time to develop new competencies.

Jesus didn't encourage us to become carpenters, but he had to make a living. He liked building stuff with wood. He appreciated quality woodworking.

Strip away my identity from the lesson, and there still remains the Universal principles of growth that ANYONE can apply to their own lives. I believe anyone is six months of personal education away from starting a business that suits them if they want to. And anyone can start changing their lives today for free right now. These life-changing principles in combination with simple but powerful breathwork meditations are what I aim to share with you in this book.

Why I Wrote This Book

A book is what saved me from suicide, and I wasn't a reader before it. Each great book I've read since has given my consciousness a level-up. I believe reading is a very practical way to change your life. I woke up five years later with a completely different life, and it started by picking up one book. Now I'm in a completely different life. A parallel Universe with better outcomes. I've got dramatically different physical, mental, spiritual, social, and economic vitality, with a compatible, beautiful girlfriend I consciously chose, and living with purpose of fulfillment and contribution. If someone like me could reconfigure their life from absolutely nothing, I know anyone can do it.

My parents were both born in Texas and grew up in migrant farm-working families. Their families settled down in California. They met and had four kids together, and I came last by 10 years, and we grew up in Dinuba, a small farm town. My family and community gave me all the support to have self-confidence and pursue my dreams of being a Christian missionary slash Rockstar. I got my brain scrambled in a car wreck at age 19, spiraled into depression, and was completely doomed to suicide by age 24. In the suicidal decision, I decided to spare my body, which is my physical identity, and kill my ego, which is my existential identity, instead. So that God could remake it how I ought to be.

Get Your Mojo Back started sometime in 2019. Enough people asked me for advice on how I became "happy again" that it made sense to write it. I had a smaller apartment at the time and my desk was overflowing with notebooks from all my research on life transformation. Writing this book was my first attempt at organizing that research, and distilling it into something helpful.

Anyone can learn what I have to teach. They are some of the governing principles of the Universe. Use them to discover your own meaning, choose the worthiest lifelong pursuits, and take action with minimal misjudgment.

Meditation and specific knowledge allowed me to rediscover life meaning, redefine my identity, and live life on my terms.

You and I are two different people with unique experiences, this is true. Yet what worked for me might work for you. I was once different than I am now, but I learned from others' experiences. If you forget about me, you should see what the Universe is trying to show you through this book in this moment.

Overcome your self-consciousness by believing you belong here, doing what you feel in your heart is true. Gain self-belief by meditating on the principles in this book. The highest meaning we can realize for ourselves is to contribute to the advancement of life and love for ourself and others using our God-given natural inclinations and attributes.

Developing lifelong pursuits will keep you alive for life. Understanding yourself is the ultimate lifelong pursuit. The reward is enlightenment. The great benefits of enlightenment are Eternal Life and Eternal Love in this life and the next.

You will never run out of self to realize. You can, if you so choose, create a lifestyle of self-realization, and that will give you continuous enlightenment. And it is available to anyone. Soon you will look over your shoulder and hardly recognize yourself. All that remains of your past self is the stories you tell. You can only change so much about the outside of your life today depending on your finances or circumstances, but you can change pretty much everything about you on the inside for free.

The paradoxes of life lay in its metaphysical nature. People find comfort in their default understanding of life until they can grow no longer, but then suffer the consequences until it's time to die. Your fate can be fortified through self-understanding. Your identity can be reordered to withstand the test of Time.

What You Will Gain From Reading This Book

Self-confidence is specific knowledge. My years of researching self-understanding has produced a system of building self-confidence that has allowed me to go from crippling depression and ruined life to a life of physical, mental, spiritual, social, and economic vitality.

Having confidence in yourself is an existential proposition. If you don't have confidence in yourself, you feel like you don't belong. To be confident in yourself is to have a sense of certainty that the Universe wants you to be here doing what you're doing. That because the Universe wants you to be here, you are free to be yourself.

Life can feel like meaningless pain. Life can seem like pointless suffering. When you're at your lowest point, deciding to end life makes more sense than anything else. Belief in the power to change is what sets you free to experience what Life really is. Even if you don't believe in God or an Intelligent Universe, you must believe that things turn around if you can just stick it out long enough.

Even if you're not at the end of your rope right now, you may notice that over time you've been picking up subconscious shame and guilt. It's watered your personality down and gotten you believe you deserve less or you're worth less than others. As a result, you're not having the experience of life you expected. And the world is actually reacting to your new lackluster persona, which reinforces it. But the negative feelings, or addictions, or bad habits that are plaguing your outcomes in life are not "you."

"The mass of men lead lives of quiet desperation." - Henry David Thoreau

Most people are not living anywhere near their potential. It's almost always due to unconscious pain limiting our self-identity. We attach meaning to every painful moment in our lives and let it define us in our subconscious. Maybe some people get lucky with a lifetime of positive reinforcement to inflate the ego. But once a paradigm-shifting life event happens, BOOM. All of a sudden your life movie takes a totally different turn. Now what?

The bad news is I'm not selling you a get-happy-quick scheme. Orienting yourself properly requires voluntary pain. It's like lifting weights for your mind and spirit. I'm selling you pain in the short term for a more pleasurable long-term experience. You're going to have to get your proverbial hands dirty. Even meditation is more like weight training; you have to stretch your mental muscles consistently in order to have a strong mind.

This book is chock-full of mind hacking concepts where I can point to actual examples where they've helped me and others. Let these chapters be your guide on the path of Mojo Development. You want that inner freedom, and you're going to get it if you stay on the path. Consciously choose to develop your mojo every day. That's how you lay a solid foundation for making the right decisions, building stronger relationships, feeling happier, and cultivating more positive outcomes in your life and those around you.

This is a short book for a reason - It's got no fluff. Reading it should be easy, fast. That's the point. Read it once a month for a year, once a week for a month, or once a day for a week. The more you consume it the more it will soak in.

Many people will live to be nearly 100 years old and never get to experience living a second life. Most people's dying regret is not chasing their dreams and living life on their own terms. Not believing in the worth of their own happiness. If you want to stop living a life of meaningless suffering. If you want to turn a meaninglessly painful life into one of self-understanding and deep existential meaning, and contribution, please keep reading.

CHAPTER 1. DEVELOPMENT

Physical Mojo Development

I was maybe 7 years old, at the Dinuba High School pool with my buddy Alex. During summer months, the high school opened the pool to the community charging one or two dollars to get in. It was my first time and I was following Alex to the diving boards. We chatted the whole way up the ladder of the high dive. I didn't realize what a huge mistake I'd made until I got to the top and Alex stopped talking.

With a cannonball, he disappeared over the edge.

Walking up to the edge set a rock in my stomach. It made me want my mommy! I turned around to chicken out and go back down, but there was a girl ready and waiting for her turn. And a line of people waiting on the ladder right behind her.

I must have been up there a while because I remember the lifeguard coming up to help me jump down. She approached me and beckoned me toward her. I took a look at her, and at that moment made a decision about fear that would affect me for the rest of my life. I decided that the shame of having to chicken out in front of the entire town's kids would be more painful than if I accidentally splatted myself into the ground. I closed my eyes and pencil-jumped.

I might not have done it again that day, but after I made that decision I knew I could at least pencil-jump. I wasn't afraid of it anymore. Better late than never. I learned my first lesson in physical mojo development.

Like Driving A Car

The first time you reach 25 miles per hour it feels like you're flying - Like you're on the edge of losing control. A year later you're texting, driving, putting on your makeup or saucing your taco bell burrito all at the same time.

Physical mojo is earned by doing. You develop confidence in that which you feel most comfortable doing. You feel most comfortable with it because you're good at it, which comes from doing it a lot. There is a room in everyone's life where they're the rockstar. When you're the only one who can fix the computer, you're the most competent person in the room. When you're the only one who can cook a brisket, you're the mojo master of the moment.

There's no age limit to increasing your physical mojo by pushing yourself into new experiences. A few years ago I randomly took up Brazilian jiu-jitsu. Because of that, I've been able to experience combat simulations nearly every day for the last four years, compete on a stage, and make so many awesome friends.

Our minds record everything we do and our consciousness translates that information into meaning.
That's why it's important to build your physical competence in various things if you want to accomplish your life's greatest desires.

The more you understand something, the more confidence you feel by doing it. The more you want to be around it. It becomes you. So pick some key things that are good for you that will naturally get you where you want to go simply by doing them. And then do them a lot.

Leverage these positive emotional states to take a small action toward something you want. Face a little fear, a micro challenge, and if you fail it won't hurt that much. You took one step out the front door. Recompose yourself and try again. Each time you fail at something, you take one step closer to success at that thing. Failure and success are not permanent positions. They're not even good resting places.

Once you get your first small success, you gain the mojo required to take the next step. And your desires increase just as fast. Every failure becomes mojo-building by nature when you realize that life is an experiment, and failure is just a sign pointing you to the next step.

Take a second to feel a sense of gratitude for everything that didn't work out in your life. They've brought you to this point where you now have thick-enough skin to take on the ultimate challenge: The challenge of self-understanding.

All the pain, suffering, desires, challenges, and rewards you've experienced have made you tough enough to get this far in life. Despite all odds. The mojo you develop from now on will help defend you against your toughest opponent of all, which is your own subconscious mind. Your own shadow. Your own ego.

Cultivating your mojo will help you realize you can take the pain. Every time you take an action that is in alignment with your highest vision of yourself, you take a stance against your weaker self. You discipline your inner child and put the whip to your subconscious mind. All difficult tasks become easy with repetition.

Mental Mojo Development

Mental mojo development is about gaining control over your mind. Mind-controlling yourself. What I refer to here as the MASTER MIND.

Creative Visualization

About 18 months into "depression recovery" I tried public speaking. Even though I felt ready because of all the personal development I had been doing, I was sick with nerves driving to the build where I was to deliver the keynote speech at a high school tech conference. Not necessarily a high-stakes endeavor, but still a good test of my ability to overcome self-consciousness and achieve comfort within the uncomfortable.

I picked an empty conference room, sat on the floor, closed my eyes and began to meditate. After a few minutes of intense breath I visualized myself walking into the room, picking up the microphone and speaking. I imagined it not going well at first, and persevering through it. My emotional state rose as I imagined myself giving the entire speech confidently. I opened my eyes, walked out of the room and straight into the conference hall.

The Point:

In a fight, the first punch surprises you the most. On a stage, the first punch is the crowd's initial response. To be successful at anything challenging, you must learn to roll with the punches. The mind is constantly trying to attach meaning to experiences based on the emotions we feel.

If we believe those narratives, we start behaving unpredictably. Creative Visualization is a technique for preparing your mind for moments of decision, or action. You use your mind to see the movie before it happens, and thus feel the feelings before they happen. It is one of my primary methods for mental conditioning.

My First Cage Match

In 2019 I accepted my first ever jiu-jitsu cage match. It was an 8-minute submission-only match, in the middle of an amateur MMA event, with over 700 people in attendance. I took the match to prove to myself that mental conditioning is more powerful than the limits of my previous experience. And to start sharpening my identity as a competitor.

I was facing someone with a higher rank and more experience, I had only one previous competition, and I had just under three months to prepare and lose 25 pounds. I used creative visualization every night after training to visualize the entire future fight day - From waking up to getting my hand raised at the end of the night.

I even made an audio track of my walkout song mixed with 8 minutes of crowd noise and set it to repeat. I imagined hundreds of possible outcomes for the match while practicing vigorous breathwork. When the day came it was like I had entered the Matrix. Everything played out almost exactly like I'd visualized. I was able to keep calm and remain in the present moment. In the locker room during warmup I was still playing the track in my earphones and visualizing myself competing naturally and comfortably. I was completely on fire for the moment as it unfolded before me.

I went the 8-minute distance with a higher-level competitor in a submission-only cage match. He took an EBI Overtime win by time limit. I didn't get the win, but we had an epic battle in a cage under bright lights. It was a personal win.

The Point:

Don't just expect yourself to show up ready to fight when it's time. Prepare for it today. Everyone has their own fight that is coming for them. Most of the time we don't have the advantage of knowing what day to expect it. Be ready.

Spiritual Mojo Development

Don't be intimidated by the concept of spiritual development. If we can develop mind and body, we can develop spirit. Consider self-confidence from a spiritual perspective for a moment.

Self-confidence is a feeling of trust in one's own abilities, function, or purpose in any given moment. What does trust in yourself feel like? Some call it intuition. Not having trust in yourself feels like you've got no compass. Without a working compass, how can there be a right path?

Mojo today isn't about who can swing their club hardest. Today, the mind kills more than sword and bullet. Self-talk can weaken any person to the point of complete self-doubt and directionlessness. Self-talk infection leads people to suicide every day.

Bruce Lee is one of the greatest manifestations of true self-confidence. He said, "action is a high road to self-confidence. Where it is open, all energy moves toward it, and its rewards are tangible."

You must believe that the Universe wants you to be here, otherwise you wouldn't be. You must understand everything you want is waiting for you on the other side of this thing holding you back. Take a walk in your own shoes for a change - Your true identity holds all the self-confidence in the world.

External influence isn't here to shape your identity or your purpose. It's here to help you shape your sword to a fine point. You have the power within you to find and uphold your own internal code. The code that is written on your soul. It is known only to you and God. It can be ignored, but not escaped.

Be Your Self.

Action Steps

Meditation for Vitality

Watch the *Meditation for Vitality* video: videos.getyourmojobackbook.com/sep

CHAPTER 2. LIFE MASTERY

"I will live this day as if it is my last. This day is all I have and these hours are now my eternity. I greet this sunrise with cries of joy as a prisoner who is reprieved from death… I will beat upon my heart with gratitude as I consider all who greeted yesterday's sunrise who are no longer with the living today… Why have I been allowed to live this extra day when others, far better than I, have departed? Is it that they have accomplished their purpose, while mine is yet to be achieved? Is this another opportunity for me to become the man I know I can be?"
— Og Mandino, The Greatest Salesman in the World

Life Mastery

All great achievers are recognized for their mojo.

Michael Jordan is a superstar example. Michael Jordan bragged about being the best, which gave us the impression of mojo. But his self-expression came from a place of inward humility. In fact, Michael Jordan was the humblest player in the entire league, because he notoriously practiced earlier and longer than anyone else. And he only practiced *the fundamentals*. He didn't believe his ego, identity, or personality made him a star. He believed we are equal and what separates us is consistent, focused effort.

"I've failed over and over again in my life, and that is why I succeed." - MJ

"I've always believed that if you just put in the work, the results will come." - MJ

"I can accept failure, everyone fails at something. But I can't accept not trying." - MJ

The only way to mock Michael Jordan is to criticize his professional baseball career. Mind you, we're talking about two pro sports careers from one person.

No matter where you slice the pie of all-time human achievers, you'll find a model of self-confidence. Start naming a few for yourself and see if it's true: Elon Musk, Andrew Carnegie, Sam Walton, Donald Trump, and Martin Luther King Jr all had it.

Anyone at the top of the charts in their field had to believe they could sustain that self-belief over time. From pro sports athletes, to artists, to tycoons, and emperors. What makes the difference between the achievers and the wishers?

Mindfulness

"The practice of paying attention to the present moment and doing so intentionally, and with non-judgment. Mindfulness meditation practices are deliberate acts of regulating attention through the observation of thoughts, emotions, and or body states." - Psychology Today

For some, mindfulness is the answer to all of life's problems. For others, mindfulness is an enigmatic term and suggests little or no implied actual technique. Mindfulness is a practical tool you can use to access your MASTER MIND.

You can practice overriding your mental programming to run a program that's more beneficial to you instead. That is the MASTER MIND ability. When you are presented with an unexpected situation, you feel initial stress and frustration. Your stress response is a good thing. The fight or flight. It is your interpretation of it that causes you the trouble.

Bring your awareness to your emotions as they change. Ask yourself why, decide which to accept or let pass. You'll naturally start realizing more empowering meanings for your emotions.

Instead of feeling panicked in the face of a new challenge, couldn't you have just as easily been excited if you weren't caught off guard? It's a choice that's happening in your mind. If you slow it down long enough to look at it, you'll see that every time.

Emotions are fleeting and don't give us accurate representations of reality. Emotions don't improve judgment. They don't improve decision making. Let the negative ones pass. Hold on to the good ones long enough to use them as fuel for action if you need it. And then let them pass, too.

Don't react to frustration, worry, or stress. When you react, you accept its meaning.

If we use fighting as a metaphor for life situations, the first punch in a fight is the initial stress response. Don't tense up. Roll with the punches before reacting. Then you can see more clearly and with more awareness to the truth of the situation. With open eyes and a calm mind you can land a clean knockout punch of your own.

Let negative emotions pass. You made a mistake? Let it go. The opportunity that corrects it and puts you in a better place is already here if you're paying attention. You can rather save that energy up for a positively-charged action. Like anything, you get better at this with practice. Fortify your emotional body. Inner peace is the byproduct of doing so.

Make every new challenge a self-empowerment opportunity. Let your breath restore your lifeforce, preparing you to restore balance to the moment.

THE GREAT RIGHT NOW

Any time you feel worried, afraid, or ashamed, you're thinking in the future or the past. Even if it feels like right now, only a potential outcome could cause worry, which is in the future. Shame feels like you've got a debt of poor reputation at stake.

In the moment right now, nobody is thinking about you and nobody cares about your past except for you. Nobody knows what you're thinking of doing in the future except for you. So any time you feel ashamed, know that it is all self-inflicted and unnecessary. To the moment, you are what you think and do and that is it.

How To Manage Negative Feelings

> *"Never let the future disturb you. You will meet it, if you have to,*
> *with the same weapons of reason which today arm you against the*
> *present." – Marcus Aurelius, Meditations*

Get focused on this critical second. Not on expectations, not on outcomes, but the Great Right Now.

When I got into a cage in front of 700 people I needed something to keep me from getting nervous too early and dumping out all my adrenaline
before the match. When I noticed myself feeling anxious or nervous, I'd tell myself things like "Hey, that's tomorrow. Today's not important enough for you? When the time comes you always know what to do." To pull yourself out of a negative emotion, focus all your energy on the present moment. You'll feel a recharge of self-confidence.

Bring your presentness ability with you everywhere you go. You'll be ready for anything.

Think about how annoying it is when someone stares at their phone the whole time they're with you. Their attention is elsewhere. Now think about the most awesome people in your life. What are they doing in your imagination? Probably paying attention to you and responding with something valuable.

Give yourself to the moment. The world will give itself back to you.

Action Steps

Meditation for Expansion

Watch the *Meditation for Expansion* video (videos.getyourmojobackbook.com)

Text summary:

Every time you get lost in your mind or your emotions, come back to this technique. Your breath is your lifeforce. USE the Force. Tune in to the MASTER MIND.

Need help with this exercise? Go to videos.getyourmojobackbook.com

Vision Mastery

All life is growth. Without growth, you have death. Without life, you have death. Death is the antithesis of growth.

If you don't use your muscles, they atrophy - Your body eats them. If your business doesn't sell product, it runs out of money and goes bankrupt. If you don't eat the vegetables, the pantry becomes stinky.

The main key to staying alive is to always have a functioning lifelong plan. Most people have a 10-year plan and they think it's a lifelong plan. When they achieve it, or it fails, they become depressed. Then they spend 10 depressed years unconsciously ruining everything they built.

Life is a long game. You decide what games you're playing - What quests you're pursuing. Then it's up to you to learn the rules. No one should tell you what to do. To live a long happy life, it's up to you to choose lifelong games with plenty of positive potential outcomes.

Take a few minutes right now with a piece of paper and pen to ask yourself *"What would I like my life to be like if nothing stopped me?"*

Write down everything that comes to mind for the following 3 minutes. You can always erase or cross things out, so just go nuts. Then ask yourself *"What would that feel like? What feelings would I have as I live my daily life?"* And write down your thoughts for another 3 minutes.

What would you do on a daily basis if your life was that way? Really imagine it and let yourself feel the emotions attached to your imagination. *"Okay, now what would I have to do from now until then to get my life to that place sometime in the next 10-20 years?"*

Write down in 5-year increments what your hypothetical plan would be to achieve this life situation.

Leave nothing unwritten. That's the secret to this: Your subconscious mind requires emotional content to create mental change. As you write it becomes more real in your mind and in your heart. Imagination is the mind's greatest talent. As with anything, you can improve your imagination with practice.

What city will you be living in? What will your family look like? Who will your new friends be? What will your bank account say? What will people say about you?

When you're reading a book about how to change your life is not the time to limit your possibilities. You can worry about the "how" later. Have fun with this.

Remember that deep down you still believe that anything is possible for you. That with one last push of all your might you can make anything happen.

DOWNLOAD THE [[VISION MASTERY WORKSHEET]]: videos.getyourmojobackbook.com

Maybe you won't drop your life as you know it right now and start living like this person tomorrow morning. It doesn't matter how long it takes, but you can start now by keeping it in the forefront of your mind. Meditate on it as you live and your actions will be shaped by it and your outcomes will be shaped by those actions. It starts with how you think. Your subconscious mind will go to work for you in small ways every day.

Your reticular activating system, R.A.S, what your brain uses to decide what to pay attention to, kicks on every time an opportunity presents itself for you to assume your new behaviors. Because it exists so strongly in your mind. Program your mind with the desire to develop your new vision.

Your path and next steps unveil before you as you discover firsthand what it is like to live with VISION MASTERY.

Death Mastery

Most people don't try new things simply because they're afraid. Afraid of what? Not afraid of dying, because almost nothing can kill people anymore.

If we're not afraid of death, then what are we afraid of? Being embarrassed, losing respect, losing our position in our job, being ostracized from our family, our church, or social circle. Social shame might be the greatest demotivator.

Why does losing the respect of our tribe matter so much to us that we avoid doing that which we love, and pursuing that which we desire, even to our deathbeds? Our subconscious is evolutionarily adapted to keep a running score of our rank in the social dominance hierarchies we participate in. We're tribal animals, what can we expect? In our indigenous hunter-gatherer days, there was always a hero of the day who brought back the most food for the village.

I've read and heard too many amazing accounts of unbearable suffering but to believe that no matter how bad someone had it as a child, no matter how much the cards have been stacked against them, no matter how hellish their life has been, every human is capable of overcoming their mind and vanquishing fear and manifesting the hero of their own life's story.

Here's the thing though: 99% of the people in your life don't know what you're capable of.

Another even more important thing: They don't care. The people closest to you don't really care what you're doing with your life. Their own life management requires almost all of their attention, just like yours. They want you to "be happy" but mostly they just want to make sure you're going to be around to pay attention to them.

This shouldn't discourage you about them. Or humanity. It should enlighten you to the realization that despite our good nature and best intentions, we are all living our own self-centered experience, so you should set your own expectations for life.

Measure your success by your own metrics and no one else's. No one is going to share a cent of your failures or unhappiness. A lofty goal you set yourself is infinitely better competition than other people and their accomplishments. Play games in life where second place doesn't feel good unless you beat your previous record. It's not about coming in first against others. It's about coming in first against your yesterday's self.

The "One-Day Life" Model Of Consciousness

Consider this "One-Day Life" Model of Consciousness as a thought exercise you can use anytime to become aware of your highest values and what behaviors would allow you to manifest those values immediately. It also has a natural side effect of increased levels of gratitude for the gift of life, which will curry you good favor with God/the Universe.

By shortening your life expectancy you receive the added benefit of considering what "getting your affairs in order" would look like.

What needs to be done for you in order to die with dignity? If you couldn't fulfill your bucket list because it turns out you're not going to live until you're 100 but your life ends today or tomorrow, how should you live so you can die with some feeling that you fulfilled a higher purpose?

If life was designed for you to figure out that you are the hero of your own life story, your own life movie, and today was the day that you finally figured it out, what would you do differently? Live like your actions today sculpt the monument your life will be remembered by forever.

Treat each day like it is your chance to show the world how excellently you've lived. You will begin to make yourself proud. Rise, fight, and return to the earth a hero. Live a mini-life each day.

> *"I will live this day as if it is my last. And if it is my last, it will be my greatest monument. This day I will make the best day of my life... My last must be my best. I will live this day as if it is my last. If it is not, I shall fall to my knees and give thanks." – Og Mandino, The Greatest Salesman In The World*

The only way to pursue your dreams is to get moving.

If you've ever considered suicide, that's your great trade secret! Imagine you've already died and this is your second life. What do you have to lose?

If you live in a country with government welfare assistance, if you have more than one person who knows you and somewhat cares whether you live or die, you have to realize that there are almost no severe consequences to going for it. What's the worst that can happen? You go bankrupt? So go bankrupt. Donald Trump went bankrupt for $900 million in 1990. He made 8 billion dollars when he came back. And became the President of the United States.

You'll go to jail? Put to death? Not likely, not in the US at least.

Maybe you'll starve to death or lose your home. If you're pursuing your desires and your dreams, it's unlikely you'll starve to death. You can sell your home, it's not the best place for your money anyway.

You can make money doing just about anything once you believe in yourself to do so. We're not afraid of the consequences of failure. We're afraid of facing our fears.

You're afraid to face the truth - We all are. Death is around the corner. That's part of the game of life. Our fears feel extremely valid. There are ways around it. Start running your own race. One that's worth dying for. Live your own life. Die with the glory you deserve.

To hell with anyone who doesn't like it. They won't be there when it's time to meet your maker. You'll be there alone with Death.

You might die tomorrow. You might live for another 100 years. Don't waste this life. You might have to reincarnate and live it again. Start living your dream life today. An inner spring of mojo wells up within you when you stop subconsciously letting outer influences control your life.

If it isn't worth doing every day, it probably isn't worth doing.

CHAPTER 3. IDENTITY

Identity

Everywhere I look I see a massive struggle with identity. Identity leads people to their doom. Identity keeps people from happiness. Identity is all that separates us. Identity is what makes us individual. Our identity is ultimately self-created, though it happens mostly unconsciously, and inherited by circumstance.

Society gives us identities: Racial identity, sexual identity, family identity, social, religious, national, career, political. We each decide for ourselves what those things mean to us. And how we'll behave accordingly.

Identities make us feel safe. We're accepted by the tribe if we have an acceptable identity. And should we die, it is something to remember us by. But identities can also limit us. Particularly when we accept them unconsciously.

For example, an identity I may not choose to accept is when I'm walking down the street and someone calls me a dumbass. But if I'm having a tough sales quarter and my boss calls me a dumbass, I might accidentally accept it and let it affect how I see myself.

I may choose to accept my identity as a male when I decide which bathroom to use. I may not accept it when someone tries to engage me in a "girls rule, boys drool" type of debate.

I may accept my identity as a human if I am stranded in the desert and a wounded rabbit hobbles by. I may forgo being "only human" if I'm encouraged to give in to some temptation that isn't to my long-term benefit.

I may accidentally accept my racial identity if someone insults a member of my blood family or my heritage. I may not accept it if someone invites me to a rights rally, or if I want pizza instead of tacos.

Your identity is ultimately what defines you.
Every decision you make defines you. Even if you just sit there doing nothing, that is definable as being someone who is sitting.

You can even make a case that your identity is what is going to kill you. If you're a chronically obese person, what's most likely to kill you? If you identify as a "son of an x" or "daughter of an x", you're sending yourself down a path.

If you're an alcoholic gambler, you might have a few ways to go, but you're not leaving much to surprise.
If you become an old person, eventually old age will kill you - That's your fault for becoming an old person. You could have invented a time machine, or an anti-aging formula. We choose how long we expect to live.

It's not just bad habits or misplaced priorities that can kill us. Many great achievers have killed themselves after accomplishing heights we could only dream. They became locked into an identity that no longer provided them with existential meaning and eventually they decided there was no way to a different life. I watched it happen to me, down to the suicide decision.

The Point:

Identity can be rewritten. Character can be workshopped. Life narrative can be changed. You are choosing and changing your path with every action, and it all starts with how you identify. Our identities are like snapshots of ourselves, but life is ever-changing.

Every day, people commit suicide and it might be always about their identity. I propose that we can negotiate with ourselves to develop a dynamic identity that can change easily to adapt to any and all changes in your life. An All-Weather Identity.

The only constant variable in anyone's identity is the eternal soul, which is inside, underneath, and permeating every layer of your paradigm. The Cosmic Record of your life that is being recorded and watched by only you and the Universe.

The following concepts are identity reconfiguration tools: Use them to redefine yourself in a way that delivers you net-positive outcomes.

A Dynamic Identity

A Dynamic Identity if we were computers would be like creating a root user permission to your own brain. With root access to your brain, you can more easily and quickly manage any subconscious dissonance.

A dynamic identity can be your spiritual identity. (For the non-spiritual, your existential identity. I mean, you at least have to admit that you exist, and not by your choosing, or you could willfully drop dead - Therein lies your relationship to what is "Life" or the "Powers That Be".)
Your spiritual identity, or existential identity, supersedes all other identities, because according to your subconscious mind it is the only one that may transcend Death. Your "spirit."

Non-dynamic identities will die with your physical body if they make it that long. Non-dynamic identities have expiration dates.

A dynamic identity evolves with you as you go. A dynamic identity allows you to change your non-dynamic identities when they get old without feeling like you're losing any life meaning. I mentioned earlier in this book that most people have 10-year goals and think they're lifelong goals.

When they reach the top position in their career, when their children all leave the house, when they go broke for the first time, or when a sudden accident changes their circumstances, they feel there's nothing left to do but wait for Death.

A dynamic identity will help you roll with life's punches without sustaining spiritual or psychological injury. A dynamic identity will protect you from accidentally becoming someone you're not. And it will allow you to create and recreate yourself wherever you are in life, at any point in your timeline.

A dynamic identity will give you a life-long approach to understanding your own consciousness. You may sit perfectly still in one place for 80 years and you would visibly age the same as if you spent its entirety flying around the world on an airplane. We travel through time regardless of how we move our matter through space.

As human beings, we are bound to the principle of change, as we cannot physically escape the dimensions of time and space. You can't resist! You are changing right before your very eyes.

The default condition of being alive is that you grow and change. How you grow, rather, in which ways, is up to you. Developing and understanding your consciousness is your individual responsibility. It is each person's Heaven and Hell, and each person's individual commission regardless of any other circumstance.

Defining Your Own Principles and Values

Most people fail in life because they major in minor things." – Tony Robbins

Everything you woke up with this morning defined you before you could even give yourself a chance to decide who to be.

We know there are millions of things going on all around us that we aren't aware of, from a molecular level to a cosmic level. We can be conscious to only a limited number of things at any given time. Even of those things, we only pay attention to the ones that make us feel something. But we can only think, say, and do based on that which we're aware of. So our entire life experience is determined by our level of awareness.

Every decision you make shapes your path as you progress through time. We chase what makes us feel good and reject what makes us feel bad. But we do so unconsciously, which tends to get us in trouble.

I propose that if you take a moment to assess your mental paradigm, you will unconsciously choose better. Since we are feelings-driven creatures, our code is to emotionally react. In order for this emotionally-reactive condition to benefit us, it is in our best interest to define to ourself who we are, what we want, and what we are doing with our time here on Earth.

In this way, we respond in alignment with our highest identity by default. We remove a significant source of conflict from our lives as we manage our internal response to external circumstance.

Don't be intimidated by this. If you want rock-solid character in real life, you can't keep it all in your head. You need to write it down. It can be as simple as making a values list or as thorough as writing your whole life story all the way from birth to what you want your obituary to say.

Values

What are you missing?

What are the feelings you prioritize over others?

Your personal values are the feelings you want more of. They're opposite of the ones you never want to feel again. Our personal values determine our principles, because we make decisions based on what we desire most.

Tony Robbins taught me that people value feelings, and the things that make them feel those feelings. Happiness, security, freedom, loyalty, vitality, love, adventure - everything you do is to secure your values.

Means

Do you value money? Or do you value the security, freedom, and the powerful feelings it gives you?

Money isn't an end, it's a means to an end. It's okay to value the means, but it is not the end. Money isn't an end value, it's a means value. Don't mistake the ends for the means in your mind or you'll end up chasing the means mistaking it for the end.

We all know someone miserable rich, with a nice house, and a beautiful family. There's always another mountain to climb. So long as you have breath, you will have desire.

Ends

Ends are the feelings the means give you. Understanding your values allows you to make accurate decisions without having to consult the angel and devil on your shoulder.

Redefine your values so that they match your vision, and your guilt and shame start to disappear. You have the ability to align your identity with a new vision at any time, so don't feel typecast into your current situation. Your new identity is a prayer and a piece of paper away.

Action Steps

- *Meditation for MASTER MIND Activation*

Watch the *Meditation for MASTER MIND Activation* video:
videos.getyourmojobackbook.com

- *Top 10 Values List*

To start, make a list. Ask yourself a few questions: *"What matters to me most? What am I willing to die for? What am I most afraid of? What do I never want anyone to have to experience ever again? What's one feeling I want everyone in the world to feel?"*

Set a timer for 5 minutes and make a list of every feeling or value that comes to mind.

You can sort them out later, just take out a piece of paper or notes and start writing.

"If I could leave my kids with one lesson, what would it be?"
"What would I do for free every day for the rest of my life if money was no object?"

My example:

1. Self-expression
2. Connection/Love
3. Intelligence
4. Creation/Invention
5. Freedom
6. Empathy/Compassion
7. Vitality
8. Adventure
9. Wealth/Resources
10. Consistency/Patience

Keep your list where you can see it on a recurring basis. Once you negotiate with the Universe how you actually want to be, become fully possessed by it. Program it into your brain by reading it daily. Even five times a day wouldn't be too much if it got you to be the "you" that you wish you were.

Take a few minutes to embody the feeling of each value and say to yourself "I am this feeling." Write a sentence or two about your thoughts on each value.

Don't forsake this practice of reading and writing about who you are. If you want to redefine yourself, do it on a piece of paper. Embody your core values, be proud of them. They are the pillars your colossus character will stand on for eternity. They are your pillars of "Self", given to you by the Universe during this time of self-reconstruction.

Resist the urge to change your list over and over. Every 10-12 months is a good check-in period. Give time a chance to do what it does best, which is to compound the interest of your investment in action.

Principles

Principles are the fundamental rules we live by to get the outcomes we desire. They are "certain truths" that, when followed, deliver a successful result. Most people function with an unconscious set of principles, with varying degrees of success. I suppose this is okay so long as they are experiencing the success.

When the success stops, it is time to ask why. I believe it was Tony Robbins who said, "When we succeed we celebrate. When we fail, we ponder." Your values determine your principles.

The unconscious rules we follow in our daily life are our principles. Our social principles show when we speak to others. Our spiritual principles show when we attend church, a yoga class, or when we are praying alone. It may be hard at first to identify what some of them are, but it may help you to start writing down your principles as you notice them occur in your daily life.

Some of my main principles I share with you in this book. I believe in them because they came from first principles of all-time greats and I continue to shape them as I apply them in my own life. Moses had 10 Commandments. Jesus had the Beatitudes. Buddha offered us several sets of "rules for life." You can bet every great achiever, leader, or ruler lives by their principles.

It may take you some time for life to give you clear perspective on your principles. But don't be afraid to make a short list right now, because you subconsciously already have them.

Don't let your default values define you - You define your default values. Don't let your default principles define you - You define your default principles.

"Some use them [their powers] to help others, to protect people. Our powers don't decide who we are. We do." – Barry Allen, The Flash

How To Expand

"Get out of your comfort zone."

Why? Why is there a comfort zone if not for us to be in it? Some part of the psyche runs calculations to determine what behaviors give us pleasure, but more importantly, which ones give us pain. The comfort zone is a framework of behaviors that we perform to avoid perceived pain. Secondarily, to reward ourselves with pleasure.

Example: Jumping off the high diving board as a kid. I wanted to climb down, but my potential death was less painful in the moment than likely humiliation.

Example: Asking out the barista at Starbucks. You want the hot date, but you'd rather not be publicly humiliated by a rejection.

Example: Asking for a raise you know you deserve. You want to get paid what you're worth, but you don't want to speak up to a perceived superior.

If you want to stay exactly how you are in this moment, remaining in the comfort zone is actually a good plan. But I doubt there is a human alive today who is 100% satisfied with everything in their life as it is and wants nothing to change. Everyone gets hungry. "Getting out of your comfort zone" means to behave in ways that are outside your normal behavior to achieve a different outcome.

The Land of Perceived Risk

The opposite of the comfort zone is the "Land of Perceived Risk".

We are comfortable with risks we know: Driving on the freeway, drinking from the glass at a restaurant, or sharing personal details with strangers. We become immediately uncomfortable around risks we don't know but have heard about: Skiing, backpacking, or investing in the stock market.

The Land of Perceived Risk is everything that's beyond even that which you don't know - In other words, what you don't know you don't know. Until you verify, any risk you assume in the Land of Perceived Risk is imaginary. There may be some, there may not.

The Land of Perceived Risk is like "The Wilderness" in the classic online role-playing game RuneScape. In RuneScape, your medieval hero character can interact, exchange, cooperate, and battle with other online players. You can't "kill" other people's characters unless you are in the Wilderness part of the map. When you die in the Wilderness, everything you bring stays behind as possible treasure for other players.

The Wilderness is home to many monsters of increasing difficulty in deeper regions of the map. Only the highest-level players can survive in the deepest regions. But low-level players still throw themselves into the deep Wilderness. They know any treasure they gain is worth the risk.

Players who haven't ventured that far have no idea what it feels like to find and own these treasures. They're more afraid to lose what little they've scraped together in the beginning than to gain new riches and experience wild adventure. And this is just a computer game.

Get out of your comfort zone and into the Wilderness of Life. You can't have the adventure from the comfort zone. You can't taste the treasure until you're in the Wilderness. Consider what "you don't know you don't know" to be the deep Wilderness. Make a habit of doing the unordinary and you prepare yourself to do the extraordinary.

Make yourself a bed in THE GREAT UNCOMMON. In other words, start doing the things you've always wanted to, but have been too afraid of the "perceived risk."

Leveling Up In The Wilderness of Life:

- Level 1: Say hi to a few strangers on the street.

- Level 3: Ask the girl at Starbucks to sit and chat with you for two minutes.

- Level 10: Ask your boss for the raise you know you deserve.
  - Book that trip to Japan.
  - Take the second job, or quit the first one.

Maybe you never go on dates because you're afraid to start a conversation with someone on the street. Maybe you're stuck in your job because you're afraid to voice your great business ideas at work. When you ignore your highest desires, you accept an outdated idea of who you are. An expired identity.

Fear becomes stronger the more we let it affect our decision-making. We are good at making excuses in the moment to justify avoiding our fears. Overthinking is simply a method we use to escape the responsibility of pursuing our desires. We overthink until the moment has passed, and then tell ourselves it wasn't meant to be.

Start small. Do something today that you wouldn't normally do. Try talking out loud in public next time you're walking down the street. Look around. Everyone is too busy being self-conscious to give you any consideration.

We are self-centered humans. Everyone sees the world as though it revolves around them. We're all looking at them, thinking about them, and whispering about them. So no need to worry about the negative social consequences of your changing behavior. They are little-to-none in reality.

In order to expand yourself, stretch your boundaries little by little. Go out of your way. If you have nothing else, the ability to free yourself from self-consciousness will give you esteem from the most admirable people. It is the one gift that money can't buy and no title can afford.

It's a skill, something that can be practiced and thus developed.

It's the mojo, baby!

Every small positive interaction you create with another person increases your mojo. Create small games for yourself to increase your mojo. Challenge yourself to stretch into your ultimate form.

Action Steps

Self-Analysis Assignment

Meditation for Aura Expansion
Watch the *Meditation for Aura Expansion* video: <u>videos.getyourmojobackbook.com</u>

    1.   Now spend 3 minutes imagining a fantasy life - Your life if it could go any way you choose. Don't stop imagining it, until those 3 minutes are finished.

    2.   Now spend 3 minutes writing it all down. Don't skip any details.

- Make a 20-year plan to get there.

  o   Make a 10-year plan to get to 20.

  o   Make a 5-year plan to get to 10.

  o   Make a yearly goals plan to get there in 5.

  o   Make a monthly objectives plan for this first year.

  o   Make a weekly schedule to get there.

  o   Make a daily schedule to get there.

Make four columns and put these parameters into them: "Vitality", "Resources", "Purpose", "Love"

Vitality: Physical, Mental, & Spiritual. Health
Resources: Money, Investments, Assets. Wealth
Love: Partner/spouse, Family, Friendships, Tribe
Purpose: Career, Business, Contribution, Empire

Now give yourself a (1-10) ranking for each category as you stand right now.

For example: My physical health right now is about 7, mental health about 7, spiritual health about 8. That's a 7 for Vitality.

Now that you know where you stand in the four categories of life, you can markedly improve. It's easy to keep track of just four categories. You improve categorically in these and you cannot help but start to thrive. Even if you stumble in one, your life will still show net-positive growth due to at least one or two of the other categories.

Example: In September 2016 I started Brazilian Jiu-jitsu with zero prior martial arts or grappling experience. In September 2019 I put on a big performance against a purple belt in an 8-minute cage match in front of 700 people.

In 2015 I started a digital marketing business. Success came and went, but 2018 was my worst financial year in business.
By the end of 2019 I had resolved all my debt, lost 40 pounds, and put on a big jiu-jitsu performance in a cage in front of 700 people.
The promoter will verify that weight cut.

Not to mention during that time I put out some cool songs, gained some awesome clients and new friends, made a lot of memories, and even selected a compatible and beautiful girlfriend.

If I had only one of those things to my name during that time, I wouldn't have felt like I had much reason to live when one of them fell off. Because the tides of my mojo were rising, I could stay afloat in stormy seas, instead of crashing into the rocks like before.

For each category, write down some practical things you can do to improve/expand. Each week, follow up. Keep a log or a small journal. Every 6 months, update your (1-10) scores.

CHAPTER 4. SOCIAL DYNAMICS

"When our freedom to have something is limited, the item becomes less available, and we experience an increased desire for it. However, we rarely recognize that psychological reactance has caused us to want the item more; all we know is that we want it. Still, we need to make sense of our desire for the item, so we begin to assign it positive qualities to justify the desire." – Robert Cialdini, Influence: The Psychology of Persuasion

Street Rules

Like telling a police officer you didn't know the speed limit, but still getting a speeding ticket, so are you responsible for any and all ignorant violations of the laws of life.

Being ignorant to the rules doesn't absolve you of the consequences of breaking them. If you don't like the outcomes you're getting in life, discover the rules to the games you are playing.

Those who win know the rules to the games being played. The only difference that separates the winners from the losers is their most consistent actions, or their habits. That's something we can each improve for ourselves.

Get In The Game

*"Because one's self-consciousness is too conspicuously present over
the entire range of one's attention, get rid of the intruding self and
apply yourself to the work to be done, as if nothing in particular were
taking place at the moment." – Bruce Lee*

If only it weren't for those pesky negative feelings about yourself! Then you could
actually get in the game. You're your toughest critic, your own worst enemy, your only
competition, and only real obstacle. That is, until you're not anymore. The way you
handle a situation is based on who you think you are in the moment and how you've
handled similar situations in the past. As your self-confidence increases, your inner voice
becomes increasingly cooperative. The tides of your inner monologue start to shift in
your favor.

It doesn't happen all at once. It's like starting a new job. On the first day, you're super
nervous because there's a new expectation for you to behave in a new way, to fit a new
role. A new identity. And it takes time to get good. You might not notice progress more
than every three to six months.

You generate positive momentum by believing in your direction. You manifest it from
within once you decide to believe the direction exists. Self-confidence is like a secret
pact between you and God that He will provide the next step for you if you step out in faith
that it'll be there by the time your foot hits the ground.

Self-Motivation

"It is unimportant what happens to you in life. What is important is what you do about what happens to you." – Lanny Bassham

It takes many more failures than most can stomach to become an all-time great. To become an all-time great and be remembered for generations, it requires more pain from failure than most people can withstand. Overcoming failure and sustaining progress is about changing what failure means to you.

Once you've done away with fear of failure you can play the game of life practically free of charge. Each failure becomes a stepping stone on the path to a greater you. Failures and mistakes are part of the process of any worthwhile goal. Being afraid to fail is silly, as you need scar tissue to have tougher skin. When you know your outcomes won't be perfect, you'll take more shots at your target.

And that's how you get better - Make mistakes , build that thick skin, and drill more repetitions.

The Momentum Equation

Your momentum in life is a simple equation: Matter (or mass) over time (or velocity.)

Angular Momentum	=	Moment of Inertia	X	Angular Velocity
L	=	I	X	ω
Linear Momentum	=	Mass	X	Velocity
p	=	m	X	v

The **X** implies simple multiplication here.

You are a form of matter; we can see that. Time is how we measure changes to matter in space. Time is how we explain what is happening to us. Your momentum is determined by you moving in a specific direction consistently over time.

Social Dynamics

It is weird slash cool that you can't tell by looking at someone what kind of life they live. The more you realize you don't know about reality the more you start to see interactions with people as windows into a vast kingdom.

Treat everyone like they might be a secret billionaire. Carry yourself like a secret billionaire surrounded by secret billionaires. Doors open for you when you treat your fellow man and woman as fellow royalty.

We've adapted to identify and assume social cues based on posture, behavior, and appearance. We make instant decisions about how people expect to be treated based on how they behave. People generally treat you with the same level of self-respect you present. You pave a road for yourself into people's hearts by treating them with respect. Like you are kings and queens. Kings recognize kings.

You can consider this as reciprocal altruism or positive reinforcement or the Golden Rule, which is to treat others how you wish to be treated. Treat others as though you Love yourself like God loves you, and as though there is no difference between them and you.

As you establish more of this Supreme self-confidence,, you appreciate more the differences of others. You begin to understand their self-consciousness. You become less self-centered as you become more self-fulfilled.

As we judge others, we judge ourselves. That diminishes our ability to act as though the opinions of others don't matter. Take comfort in the promise of your highest identity.

When you feel challenged, remember why you are here. If you're not sure why you are here, take some time to observe how amazing is the simple fact that you are here. Use mental effort to attune your full attention to the present moment and enjoy its raw nature. Then relay your true identity to your external environment. When you are no longer preoccupied with internal fear and shame, you can masterfully pierce through the veil of others' self-consciousness.

Self-Image

The hero's nature is inside all of us. It is embedded in our ancient brains from the days of hunting and gathering when we yearned to be the tribe hero of the day. Maybe your last memory of your hero-self is from early childhood. But it is innate in us as humans, and it is time for you to accept your hero self-image again.

At some point we fail hard enough or long enough to believe we are inadequate. At some point we start believing in the illusions of our circumstances. You showed up on Earth with the same kit as everyone else: Body, mind, and soul. Your body is aged by your behavior and environment but your mind is largely influenced by conditions beyond your conscious awareness.

Anyone who is "living the dream" has had to redevelop their mental framework to rid themselves of limiting beliefs and detrimental habits that kept them from taking right, consistent action. The super-successful consciously iron out their mental framework with coaching, education, consulting, and conditioning to make themselves even more likely to sustain success.

If life was designed for you to figure out that you are the hero of your own life story, your own life movie, and today is the day that you finally realize that, what would you do differently?

Maybe you can't imagine it. Don't worry - Just start working on your mojo one small step at a time. Your progress will have a compounding effect, like a snowball rolling down a hill. The bigger it gets, the faster it grows. Your weaknesses and failures can't oppress you when you're constantly seeking opportunities to grow. When you get your butt kicked, celebrate. Don't let it happen again. But if it does, be grateful for that one, too.

To manifest your ultimate form, you can't keep being afraid to be big. You have to believe you deserve to be here and that you have every right to fulfill your greatest desires, and that it is in fact what God wants you to do.

That's the recurring theme in this entire book: Self-confidence comes from having faith that because you exist, God wants you to exist, and because you have desire, God wants you to fulfill that desire. And acting on that faith every day until you become walking confidence - Or in other words, the Mojo Master.

CHAPTER 5. RULING YOUR KINGDOM

"Each time we face our fear, we gain strength, courage, and confidence in the doing." – Theodore Roosevelt

The Kingdom

A necessary phase in your evolutionary process is for you to believe that you can and should adapt to your changing environment. That is the prime rule of natural selection - That which is useful survives. That which isn't, doesn't. Define what's most true about you to your external environment, or you won't survive.

Like a deer must define itself in nature as fast, strong, and intuitive in order to avoid being eaten, like an owl must define itself in nature as vigilant, wise, and exacting in order to take many lives and survive, so must you define yourself as a human that is adaptable to any circumstance.

Your Kingdom must be ruled! As you rule your Internal Kingdom, your External Kingdom will yield itself to you.

Objective Worldview

Developing an objective worldview is essential for yielding positive outcomes in your social environment.

Humans are pack animals. We need each other, and we thrive the more connected we are to our tribes.

Objectivity is a method of observation and critical thinking that allows you see everyone's perspective more clearly and make more effective decisions based on those observations.

I have heard it said that there is no such thing as true objectivity, but never when talking about the individual - only when talking about social and political conflict. Personal objectivity is a powerful tool of reasoning that you can use to make better decisions with minimal misjudgment.

Benefits of Objective Thinking

Be assertive with your expectations, but don't worry about the outcomes.

No matter how smart rich famous and well-loved you may become, you're liable to a paradigm shift at any time. You are one node in a network of 7.5 billion others. That network is interwoven with countless other networks on Earth. Your consciousness is only one point of view. Every single person has their own frame of consciousness that is entirely different from yours, yet equal in complexity.

We are the smartest monkeys on Earth playing games with our time here. We're all dumb about most things. The smartest people in the world are only smart about a handful of things. Once you determine what are your lifelong pursuits and how you'll approach them, you're free from having to know everything. When you start becoming the master of the few things that make you-you, you stop feeling like you need to have all the answers.

It doesn't harm you to admit what you don't know. Your genius is non-comparative with other people's genius. The external world becomes a life of free samples to the ones who practice the Art of Being Yourself. Your ego stops competing with the world, and starts competing against your HIGHEST POTENTIAL. It sets itself to harvesting all new knowledge towards your highest benefit. You'll find there's something to learn from a 5-year-old and from your most competitive peers alike.

This is just a taste of the power of developing an objective worldview.

Defense Against Criticism, Self-Judgment

The way we respond to incoming stimulus is never unbiased. We each come from our own unique heritages, childhoods, and environmental circumstances. Before you pass judgment on those who criticize you, remember that you are lucky not to be possessed with their negative energy.

As the old adage says: "There, but for the grace of God, go I." Life could be worse for you, as you could suffer the type of pain that causes people to act in even more hateful and frightened ways than you. You can't change others as easily or effectively as you can change your own perceptions and understanding. You will not be so easily hurt by other peoples' criticisms the more you realize that their outbursts are a reflection of their inner self-judgment.

You don't need anyone to validate your existence, your identity, or your value. Build your house on firm foundations - Your vision, your principles, your highest values. Every person with true self-confidence is Lord of their Internal Kingdom.

Kings recognize kings. You stand on equal footing with any other human on Earth so long as you believe it so. For each person there is a unique perspective, but all originate from the same place of wanting to be seen, heard, and contribute to the tribe on some level. Significance in our tribe is something we all seek. Consider this before you judge others as good or bad or right or wrong. It may be the difference between a life-changing opportunity and a life-changing obstacle for you.

Attachment

"He who acts, spoils; he who grasps, lets slip." – Lao Tzu

The Cure for Disappointment

Let go of your idea of what should be, and you will never be disappointed. Buddha teaches that attachment is the key to all suffering. To worry about future or past scenes keeps us from reality as-is, which prevents us from making accurate and effective decisions.

The Sin of Attachment

Attachment is direct distrust in God as the guide of your experience. That you must know better than God what is best for you. Maybe you don't believe in God, but you must believe that the laws of Nature that have been at play for our 20,000 lifetimes have been fairly constant for us.

You're not the first person to experience a lifetime of want and suffering. Accept that things are simply happening. Meaning isn't God's to decide, but yours. That's the whole fun in the game of life is the open-ended gameplay.

Your mind is a biased judge. It's human to want to improve, but don't bet your happiness on the outcomes because you don't have to. Life itself is worthy of happiness. You don't need to do anything to be happy but practice realizing LIFE.

Attachment in Relationships

Attachment keeps us in states of quiet desperation. The more you cling to your relationships, the more it may feel they're slipping away from you. Let people flow in and out of your life as freely as you can manage.

You must learn to observe yourself. You attract people to you when you are in the flow of life. You are in the flow of life when you are free from your attachment to things that are transitory, or temporary. People are magnetically drawn to positive people. Why? It is because we are electromagnetic creatures. To explain, look at an electron cloud in an atom.

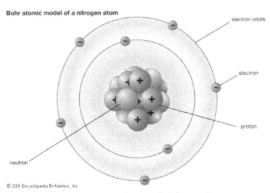

(Bohr atomic model image)

The electron cloud forms orbitally inside the atom around the nucleus, communicating electronic messages to other atoms for the rest of your system to respond accordingly. No matter how hard I try to touch you, I can't. I can only touch your electron clouds. Your electromagnetic repulsion field.

Don't doubt you are electromagnetically emitting waves other people can detect, because we are all made of them. When you're in harmony with yourself, your electromagnetic frequency emits positive polarity. To create this positive charge within yourself, feel grateful for the experience of life itself. This moment, right now. Grateful to be nominated for another day of this great gift of life.

You wouldn't worry about what others think of you if you realized
how seldom they do." – Samuel Johnson

Improving Your Speechcraft

Speechcraft is an absolutely essential skill to develop in order to have multiple positive outcomes in life and it doesn't even matter what you do for a living. If you daily speech in any way determines your income, then it totally determines it. If it determines any of your social outcomes, it determines all of them.

If there's anything magic about being a human, it's that you can speak and life as you know it can be changed. It's that you can say some words and it can cause Heaven or Hell on Earth.

Every great rise to power and power-shift in human history has come from someone's ability to speak their thoughts concisely with conviction. Power doesn't discriminate between good and evil. That's why if you want good to thrive, you must become a master of speech and use your new superpower for good.

Practice Your Speechcraft

You might have to start practicing with your own friends groups at first. Having mature, honest conversations with people is a great way to practice expressing yourself and stress-testing your principles. Realize you can relate to anyone on some level. We were all in kindergarten class together at one point. Practice expressing your true nature.

Most people have empathy they want to use, so let them use it on you by sharing your humanity with them. There's nothing people want more than a little empathy. It's easy to settle differences when two people truly understand each other. Use your mojo to lead open, honest conversations about the most important things. Great secrets of life come to you when you make a conscious effort to communicate better with people. As tribal animals, our social life is a vital component of our conscious reality. Master your socialization ability.

Speechcraft skills can be studied and practiced with measurable improvement – Things like negotiation, observation, persuasion, sales, public speaking, writing, and networking. You're going to be alive too long for you to ignore getting good at speechcraft. It'll make you a character that is worthy of respect from any one of the most refined and accomplished individuals in your world.

Say Less, Mean More

"Those who know, do not speak. Those who speak, do not know."
— Lao Tzu, Tao Te Ching

By giving, we receive more than we ever could take by force. People pleasers and domineering personalities alike often share the same misfortunate social experience: Talking a lot is a sign of weakness to people who aren't very social. It's important to know who you're talking to, and what style of communicating they prefer.

People pleasers often say more than they have to and agree more to make others feel comfortable. It's a good way to make friends, but a good way to get taken advantage of when it comes time to slice the pie. Domineering A-type personalities machine gun their way through conversations and are oblivious why they don't get invited to parties.

Both types of communicators should practice being more reserved. Let conversations run cold without feeling guilty, or fear of missing out. Don't break tension when things get awkward. Not every conversation needs to be won. Not everyone needs to like you.

We fill every moment of silence with chatter and wonder why The Universe won't answer our questions. Become a listener. Listeners are learners.

"Psychotherapy research shows when individuals feel listened to, they tend to listen to themselves more carefully, openly evaluate and clarify their own thoughts and feelings."
— **Chris Voss**

Get Comfortable With Awkward

The reason why getting comfortable with awkward moments is important for both people pleasers and domineering conversationalists is because the urge to speak is the urge to break tension and validate yourself. [SEP] The world is full of stimulus. We get caught up in the whirlwind of reaction. [SEP] When you speak or act in effort to validate yourself, you give your power to the environment. [SEP] If you were a secret prince, or princess, would you be requesting validation from your peers with the way you talk? Or the things you do with your time? [SEP] The Universe knows who to reward based on their behaviors.

Behaviors are led by thoughts. Control of thinking can be practiced. Thus, it can be improved. [SEP] Practice your mind control. Let awkward be. [SEP] Become comfortable with awkward.

Manage Your Time, Manage Your Peace

Confident people value their time more than they value what others think of them. They value what is aligned with their highest vision and don't waste their time on things, people, conversations, or thoughts that dilute their potential to achieve that vision. [SEP] We are walking on quantum threads of spacetime. You have to be willing to walk away from anything that threatens your timeline.

Your time increases in value when you have something to do with it. [SEP] You will see who is wasting your time by observing more instead of projecting. Observe those who don't respect their own time, for they won't respect yours. Beware of those who don't respect others, for they won't respect you. [SEP]

Let yourself get to a vantage point where you are safe from an iller fate. Then you can go back and help these people in the future if you so choose. [SEP] Find out specifically why you're afraid to be yourself 100% when you're at work, around friends or engaged in certain activities. Then, rule that thing out. If it's a feeling, a situation, or a person putting you down every time you open up, remove it from your life. [SEP] It's best not to retaliate unconscious attacks. It won't make you feel better, it won't make you look better, and you won't regain the time you spent being hurt by them in the first place. Accept instead that it was your fault for letting someone offend you whose opinion should mean much less than you to your own. [SEP]

Standing up for yourself isn't always a punch back. Realizing that people are mostly overgrown children, asleep to their behaviors, and walking away from a situation or relationship is much more advantageous. And it improves your life immediately. You might not get the sweet satisfaction of seeing your opponent realize it. They eventually become aware of their own unconscious pain-behavior.

Practice Your Speechcraft. Take its improvement seriously. Your ability to speak is your ability to create change for yourself and for the world.

> *"Remember, the only thing to fear is Fear, well, don't even fear Fear, for he's a cowardly chap at the best, who will run if you show a brave front."*
> — *William W. Atkinson, Thought Vibration*

On Having Friends

As you groom your Internal Kingdom from unconscious living, it becomes time to groom your External Kingdom. The people closest to you have the greatest subconscious effect on you. Your closest friends indoctrinate you with some of your unconscious biases and beliefs. They influence what you believe possible based on how they perceive themselves in relation to the world.

If you're trying to get an executive promotion and all your friends are unemployed, it's going to be a lot harder for you than for your competition, who may have friends in the industry or multi-million-dollar business owners. They're going to have a different view of what is possible, what to expect from themself, and how high they should set their goals. Your competition will feel more comfortable and sound like it in an interview because they're being given sound advice.

The best thing about having friends is you don't need that many of them. The second-best thing is you hand-picked each of yours, so you can always find new ones who naturally improve your life. Make friends with people who influence your new vision and highest ideals, and spend more time with them. You don't need to abandon your childhood friends; it might be best not to (for your lifelong story arch.) But be smart about it. And definitely be smart about your time because it's all we really have control over. Time and space.

There's a TEDx talk that Tai Lopez gave sharing his social rule of 33% and I have found it is very useful. The basis of this rule is that by spending 33% of your time with people who are 10-20 years above you who can mentor you, 33% with people at your same level, and 33% with people who you can mentor and give advice, you become a constant reciprocal of positive value. The people who are 33% above you can benefit from you because they need to pass their knowledge on.

Be self-aware enough to know what relationships you need to be the student or the mentor. However you decide the makeup of your friendships, make sure they each respect your "G-Code." That's your gangster code, the unspoken but Universal laws amongst gangsters, and it's the level of trust you should expect from your gang.

Take a minute to write down your own code of ethics you desire your friendships to follow. It's a "social design" exercise. What's the harm? See how your current friendship circle stacks up.

Sample "G-Code"

- No snitching (tattle-telling.) Absolute confidentiality.
- No discouragement. Discouragement is not productive. You'd be better off by not reaching out to this person.
- Watch each other's backs. Accountability is key. Don't let the other slack or stumble. Be the eyes behind the head. You know each other's goals and unique skillsets.
- Look out for each other's opportunities. Your inner friendships ought to be symbiotic relationships that further your development and theirs. Otherwise your time is better spent alone. Texts and phone calls will do for those who don't come with good news or gifts.

Having friends with strengths that are your weaknesses will often erase obstacles that would've otherwise prevented you from unseen opportunity. Having right friends gives you an opportunity to show them the Godhood in themselves, and for them to remind you of yours when you need it.

Life is the movie playing in your mind. The movie is being directed by the ego. Without the movie, (or ego,) we're basically deer. Your inner narration determines how you interpret reality and how you navigate your way through it.

Friendships can be serious fortifications to your life plan. They can influence you with positivity and key insights about yourself and the world from a leveraged perspective. You should be too busy doing good things to manage more than a handful of close friendships. The less your friends feed your ideal simulation the further out in your web they should be.

You really should be your own best friend. If you're married with kids, find a little time each day to get away and meditate alone. You can't avoid yourself forever. Only you will be there alone with Death in the end.

"Never waste valuable time, or mental peace of mind, on the affairs
of others—that is too high a price to pay."
— Robert Greene, 48 Laws of Power

CHAPTER 6. FEAR, FAILURE, DEATH

"If you are distressed by anything, the pain is not due to the thing itself, but to your estimate of it; and this you have the power to revoke at any moment." – Marcus Aurelius, Meditations

Your Relationship With Failure

What's holding you back from attaining your desires? What causes you to work tirelessly and be always without enough? You have unfulfilled desires, and you estimate a certain amount of suffering is required in order for you to have them. Whether it's time, money, or experience, a level of pain is all that separates you from your greatest desires.

The meaning you give pain will determine your outcomes in life. Good News! You determine your own relationship with failure. Failure is just one of two outcomes in every opportunity. It doesn't have to negatively affect your self-image. That's your choice each time.

Maybe that's not the same perspective you were given by your parents, a former sports coach, or school teacher. But maybe it's not their fault! They were just as likely to be taught by someone who was afraid of failure. If not more so than us, because the previous generations had it rougher and thus could afford less risk tolerance. It is our individual responsibility to sort out our own individual paradigm, since no one will suffer the ultimate consequences of your fears and failures but you.

Natural Selection

Let us not forget that natural selection is at play, and if we want to be the surviving mammal in this lifecycle we must overcome mind, which has become far more lethal to today's man than bullet, sword, and lion.

Your expectations of a new situation determine whether its outcome is positive or negative. The result isn't the real outcome. Everyone involved will experience it differently. Your emotional response to the result is the real outcome, because it's what can create change. And that's something you can actually control. When we feel a new incoming emotion, we think "what is this supposed to mean?" When we fail, the first thing we do is seek "what does this mean about me?"

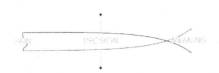

Failure doesn't mean the lion devours you, but we are still programmed to react to it that way. Your most destructive failures may land you in jail, disabled, homeless… but many felons and homeless today will still live long lives. Humans are resilient, hard to kill, we even have built-in mental safeguards against suicide. Life is a gift. No matter where you are in it. With breath, and consciousness, each day is another chance at redemption.

Champion wrestlers must be pinned thousands of times in training to be undefeated in competition. Failure is like a gift of dying without having to die. Failure is the human's metamorphosis. As Bruce Lee once said: "What is defeat? Nothing but education; nothing but the first step to something better."

No one hates failure more than a true winner. That's why winners make failure their ally. Developing a healthy relationship with failure, you'll no longer attach your identity to it. You no longer fear it. No one will tell you more than champions about the importance of failure. Michael Jordan once said, "I've failed over and over and over again in my life. And that is why I succeed."

At a local jiu-jitsu tournament once I overheard a black belt competitor saying "competition is awesome, man. I love getting my ass kicked." This particular black belt competes worldwide. Of course he loves winning or he wouldn't go to such extremes. And I know he does win often. He simply isn't afraid to lose. He doesn't allow a loss to negatively affect his identity. Whether you agree or not with his philosophy of being okay with losing, you can't deny his results as a winning black belt competitor. He also runs a large, very successful jiu-jitsu academy.

Fear of failure is far more detrimental to success than any actual failure itself. An optimistic take on failure is all you need to start realizing how to succeed. Better questions to ask yourself rather than "what does this mean about me?" are things like 'what actually happened?' And 'what can I do better next time?"

The Power of Grace

It's hard to conceptualize how long life really is. If most of us live to 60, 70, 80 years, it's to your benefit to realize that people in your life aren't going anywhere. The people you went to grade school with - A portion of them will die early, but the rest will remember you for the rest of your life. If you give people bad experiences your whole life, you'll die with a world full of enemies. Give people grace, even when they wrong you, so you can die with peace.

A former business partner slash client betrayed me on a big deal few years ago, and it was at a time when I really needed the money. I invested lots of time and resources into his project (on a handshake, because we'd done close business together for years.) Instead of paying me when I delivered, he decided to ghost me out of the blue. I reached out for months in various ways, he never responded. Instead of getting a hearty revenge, which I easily could have done, I forgave him. I finished with letting him know he was forgiven, but that I could obviously no longer call him friend. It wasn't until I told him he lost my friendship that he finally responded with an apology. So you see, even for someone who trades friendship for money, shame is the only comeuppance.

Success is impossible when you knowingly do wrong, because knowingly doing wrong adds subconscious shame to your self-image. The valuable lesson for you to learn here is there is power in having grace for yourself. In the same way, there is power in having grace for people in your life. Help people see that failure is just a part of growing. You can make up for an immature past by helping others today.

Develop your mojo, and take responsibility for the mojo of your tribe. Everyone around you is going to make mistakes. Family, friends, coworkers, employees, and loved ones. We're all learning. Give people in your life the space and time to rectify their mistakes. How do you give space and time? Have grace in your heart for them when you are talking to them. Hear them out with love in your heart. Forgive them. Teach them.

Life is long. Keep grace in your life so that people are evolving with you instead of turning from you. And should they turn from you, they can't say without lying to themselves and to God that you are anything less than a man or woman of self-confidence and grace.

"By fighting you never get enough, but by yielding you get more than you expected." — Dale Carnegie, *How to Win Friends and Influence People*

The Greatest Story Ever Told

The greatest movies, books, and songs have never told a better story than your very own. Your life in the end won't actually make sense to anyone but you. Maybe you're in a sad scene right now. Maybe it's been a long scene. How is it going to end? Unless someone's got a gun to your head right now, you'll need your imagination to answer that. Because You are directing your own life movie.

You are the director of your life. The architect of your own destiny. The scientist of your life's great experiment. Write down your goals. Journal your progress. Record your processes. Keep a journal. A video diary. Some record of the journey of your life. If you don't, who will? If you won't start now, then when? Do you want to satisfy your desires systematically, or by chance? Don't leave it to God to decide, when decision is God's gift to man! The ability to decide your meaning is at-hand.

Document your life, think through your goals and solidify your vision in writing. Each time you write it down the mental grooves become deeper. You're convincing yourself who you are and where you're going. Starting gets you halfway there.

Prioritize self-reflection: Check in on your daily, weekly, monthly, quarterly, yearly, and long-term goals. Before bed and early morning is a good time to journal about your progress and perspective and review your goals. Don't obsess and stress over it, but do value it highly.

In Lanny Bassham's highly influential book *With Winning in Mind* he describes how he used creative visualization to win six Olympic gold medals in shooting, spending more time visualizing than actual practicing. Visualize yourself manifesting your highest ideals and fulfilling your greatest goals, paint them out thoroughly in your mind, watch them play out as scenes with every variation, and let them excite you.

Write down the actions you plan to take every day, week, month, quarter, and year to make your desires become reality. Writing it down makes it real. If you don't write it down, you won't have a record of the epic progress you're about to make.

MEASURE YOUR PERSONAL KPI'S (KEY PERFORMANCE INDICATORS) - THE THINGS THAT MAKE YOUR GOAL IMPORTANT. IF YOUR LIFE WAS A MULTIMILLION-DOLLAR BUSINESS OPERATION, WHAT DATA WOULD YOU BE MEASURING? WHAT GOALS WOULD YOU BE TRACKING? IF YOU'RE THE BOSS, HOW WOULD YOU REPORT THAT DATA TO YOU? TAKE YOUR LIFE SERIOUSLY AS YOU WANT IT TO BE. TREAT YOUR LIFE LIKE IT'S A MULTIMILLION-DOLLAR MOVIE PRODUCTION, BUSINESS, OR WAR CAMPAIGN.

Videos.getyourmojobackbook.com

He Who Must Not Be Named

Notice how everyone was afraid to say Voldemort's name in Harry Potter? They'd never seen him. But he killed people they knew. The only ones who used his name were ones who'd confronted him. Only those who have seen it and been touched by it are comfortable with Death.

Fear is pain telling us to avoid failure. Our senses guide us away from pain and toward pleasure. So fear of failure is a pain response to our idea of what failure means.

Failure means more pain. Rejection, shame, guilt, poverty, and descent down the social dominance hierarchy are the possible negative outcomes of failure. That's not where it stops, though. Pain left untreated becomes worse pain, called suffering. Suffering becomes unbearable and further untreatable the longer it lasts. Eventually enough pain and suffering means death.

Pain is death knocking. We've been avoiding it all our lives. Unfortunately, our brains are old technology telling us we're more vulnerable than we really are. Death is inevitably coming. Pain is a voluntary opportunity to explore death while you're still here.

Face Voldemort behind bulletproof glass. Observe your fears and conquer them with love for life itself. Just like Harry Potter's mom's self-sacrificial love, called "deeper magic", protected him from Voldemort, the personification of Death, and his death curse.

"Shall I divulge how I truly lost my powers? [Whispers] Yes, shall I? It was love. You see, when sweet, dear, Lily Potter gave her life for her only son, she provided the ultimate protection. I could not touch him. It was old magic, something I should have foreseen." –
Voldemort to Harry Potter, Goblet of Fire (2005)

Action Steps

Meditation for Overcoming Depression

Failure is Fear's little brother. Fear is Death's little brother. [SEP] If you want to overcome your fear of failure, fear of living, fear of dying, you can meditate yourself through it. [SEP]

Watch the *Meditation for Overcoming Depression* video:
videos.getyourmojobackbook.com [SEP]

Meditation isn't just about emptying your mind.
Meditation is a spiritual chamber where you spirit can be free from the limitations of being connected to your body and two eyes. [SEP]
Imagination and intuition are products of the mind-spirit connection. [SEP]
When your spirit is free, your imagination and your intuition can receive exercise.
There is time for quieting the mind, and there is a time for exercising it.
Meditation is the appropriate space for both. [SEP]
Bring your attention to death, as you fear it.
Bring your attention to pain, as you fear it.
Your mind is the great simulation room, powered by the Imagination.

CHAPTER 7. CONCLUSION

"You are the director of your life. The architect of your own destiny.
The scientist of your life's great experiment."
- Anthony Polanco

I wrote Get Your Mojo Back to be a practical handbook, a resource for you to learn more about you. The concepts in it I derived from studying all-time great achievers, philosophers, and leaders, and practicing their discovered first principles in my own life.

Though you and I are similar in many ways, we are having two completely unique experiences. My story is still being written. I only include personal details because you need to know that I am human. My being any particular identity has little to do with my outcome. If I lived a hundred lifetimes, I could come to this conclusion a hundred different ways.

People starting worse off have done even greater things than I. And someone has probably written a better book about it. Still, if these pillars keep me in the proverbial "seat of ascension" then I feel obligated to share it with you. It was Seneca or Aurelius who said, "Think of yourself as dead. You have lived your life. Now take what's left and live it properly."

This life of mine is a free pass, so I'm going to use it to serve others. What can I do to help? I can share my experience. Who else knows that better than me? You are the expert of your own experience. Who knows you better than you? Share what you know. Maybe it'll help someone. If it helps one person, isn't it worth it? If it helps one person, wouldn't it likely help a hundred?

Leaning On The Tribe

Several amazing humans in my life would have to be better than angels, because they showed up day after day to help keep me on the path of life.

My buddy Justin was always there for me, but particularly grateful for those lowest points. Justin would drag me along with him whenever he could manage to get me out of the house. Constantly coming over and getting me to hang out was really keeping me from checking out for good.

My mom and dad have always been too loving for my own good. They didn't know how to help, but they were still there checking in on me. My mom is the one who set me up with a therapist when I needed it. She and I were always close, but she saved my life with that. I only felt comfortable telling her I was suicidal because of our friendship. My parents cared for me even though they didn't have to, and helped me out way more than they should have. They are pure-hearted, selfless folks.

The writings of classic philosophers and biographies of humanity's all-time greats helped shape my paradigm and I would thank these people if I could. I owe these sages a large debt of gratitude as well. They helped me along during the darkest times as I began my ascent from the depths of mental chaos. It felt like they were there with me.

I include this section because I messed my life up a lot, over a long period of time, and still there were some humans who decided to be there for me, anyway. We need people. We come from one original tribe and we want to be contributors to our tribe and we strive to be hero of the day, even if unconsciously. A simple word from a stranger can save your life when you're getting ready to check out for good. I'm so thankful for these characters in my life who, despite my worst efforts, helped preserve my life.

Parting Thoughts

Live the life God intended for you. Develop your self-confidence and be the freeform expression of yourself. To cultivate your mojo is a practice of personal development from a spiritual perspective. Believe in the harmony of your vision with God's Will for your life. Keep readjusting your vision as you progress until this harmony is 100% true.

Remain steadfast in your principles and values. The tides of your mojo will ebb and flow as you traverse spacetime. Use the techniques and principles in this book to regain your mojo in times of uncertainty and stress.

Draw upon your faith to dream. Believe in the power of your imagination, which is your God-given inheritance. Imagine yourself the way God intended you. Write it down like you're writing for God and translating His thoughts on your piece of paper. Outline the principles and values you would need to live by. Live by them as you march through spacetime toward your ultimate Truth. May you understand your Self through persistent, honest seeking, and find ever-increasing love and peace there.

For more resources on how to Get Your Mojo Back, visit videos.getyourmojobackbook.com. To contact me directly: Anthony@godxp.com

ABOUT THE AUTHOR

ANTHONY POLANCO is a music artist, digital marketing consultant, and former Christian missionary. He is the founder of GodXP Self-Understanding, a personal development company.

Anthony's pursuit for spiritual understanding started as an 11-year-old Christian missionary. He evangelized in Kenya, Africa for a month with a small ministry team and no family. At age 15, Anthony started a Christian metal band with his friends, and within the year were booked for a performance for Vans Warped Tour's Fresno event. He spent his high school years writing and performing music and graduated from Dinuba High School in 2009. At age 19, 7 days before a ministry trip, he was in a violent head-on collision while driving midday and woke up in a hospital bed two hours later. What followed was a 5-year chronic depression and existential crisis leading to suicide ideation at age 23. He devoted the next 6 years to researching personal development and spiritual understanding and testing in his own life by starting a digital advertising business, competing in Brazilian Jiu-jitsu, performing original solo music, and studying yoga meditation before writing and publishing "Get Your Mojo Back" in February 2020.

Anthony Polanco's research and work are inspiration to many suffering existential crises and existential depression. For videos, writing, and music, visit anthonypolanco.com.

RECOMMENDED READING

You are invited to read any of my materials on Anthonypolanco.com and GodXP.com and my YouTube channel for more on personal development, spiritual enlightenment, depression recovery, and other related topics.

In addition, the following books have been quintessential in my personal development and I recommend them for you:

- The Greatest Salesman In The World by Og Mandino
How To Win Friends and Influence People by Dale Carnegie
- The Science of Getting Rich by Wallace D. Wattles
- Meditations by Marcus Aurelius
- Influence: The Art Of Persuasion by Robert Cialdini
- Think and Grow Rich by Napoleon Hill
- Mind Hacking by John Hargrave
- Autobiography of a Yogi by Paramahansa Yogananda
- The Essays of Ralph Waldo Emerson
- Money: Master the Game by Tony Robbins
- Thought Vibration by William Walker Atkinson
- Studies in Pessimism by Arthur Schopenhauer
- Man's Search for Meaning by Viktor Frankl
- The Art of War by Sun Tzu
- The Prince by Niccolò Machiavelli
- Sell or Be Sold by Grant Cardone
- Tao Te Ching by Lao Tzu

One Last Thing…

If you enjoyed this book, please leave a review on Amazon or the store where you purchased it. I know your time is extremely valuable, and I greatly appreciate your support, and it will go a long way. Thank you.

NOTES

— Marcus Aurelius, Meditations: Marcus Aurelius, Emperor of Rome, 121-180. The Meditations of Marcus Aurelius. Mount Vernon [N.Y.] :Peter Pauper Press, 1942. 58

— William W. Atkinson, Thought Vibration: Atkinson, William Walker. The Law of Attraction: Thought Vibration. N.p.: Theophania Publishing, 2011. 55

"action is a high road to self-confidence. Where it is open, all energy moves toward it, and its rewards are tangible.": https://brucelee.com/podcast-blog/2019/1/15/133-action-as-medicine... 22

"The mass of men lead lives of quiet desperation." - Henry David Thoreau: Thoreau, Henry David, and Jeffrey S Cramer. 2009. The Maine Woods. New Haven: Yale University Press. . 17

"Think of yourself as dead. You have lived your life. Now take what's left and live it properly." - Marcus Aurelius 64

"He who acts, spoils; he who grasps, lets slip." — Lao Tzu: Laozi. Tao Te Ching. New York :Vintage Books, 1972. 51

"Never waste valuable time, or mental peace of mind, on the affairs of others—that is too high a price to pay."
— Robert Greene, 48 Laws of Power: Greene, Robert, and Joost Elffers. 2000. The 48 Laws Of Power. New York, New York, U.S.A: Penguin Books... 57

"Psychotherapy research shows when individuals feel listened to, they tend to listen to themselves more carefully, openly evaluate and clarify their own thoughts and feelings."
— Chris Voss: Voss, Chris., Raz, Tahl. Never Split the Difference: Negotiating As If Your Life Depended On It. United States: Harper Business, 2016. 54

"Some use them [their powers] to help others, to protect people. Our powers don't decide who we are. We do." — Barry Allen, The Flash: "True Colors." The Flash, Season 4, episode 18, Warner Bros., 6 Feb. 2018 40

INDEX

GodXP Publishing

READ THIS BOOK IF YOU ARE READY TO IDENTIFY YOUR EXISTENTIAL MEANING, LIFE PURPOSE, AND BECOME THE DIRECTOR OF YOUR LIFE.

GET YOUR MOJO BACK IS A DEPRESSION RECOVERY HANDBOOK FILLED WITH TECHNIQUES.

CONCEPTS AND PRINCIPLES DESIGNED TO HELP YOU BUILD A NEW CHARACTER FOR YOURSELF.

DEPRESSION CAUSES EXISTENTIAL CONFUSION. THIS BOOK IS A GUIDE TO COURSE CORRECTION.

A DEVOTIONAL GUIDE TO EXISTENTIAL IDENTITY RECONFIGURATION.

A DISTILLATION OF TECHNIQUES, CONCEPTS AND PRINCIPLES USED TO RESHAPE YOUR IDENTITY

AT ANY POINT IN YOUR TIMELINE. PUT YOUR EXPERIENCE INTO A COMPREHENSIVE STRUCTURE

OF PRINCIPLES THAT YOU CAN USE TO NAVIGATE AND BECOME THE DIRECTOR OF YOUR LIFE.

IF YOU'RE STRUGGLING TO MOVE FORWARD IN LIFE. EACH ONE OF THESE PRINCIPLES ARE

BATTLE-TESTED AND READY FOR YOU TO UTILIZE. YOU ARE THE ARCHITECT OF YOUR DESTINY.

THE SCIENTIST OF YOUR LIFE'S GREAT EXPERIMENT.

GET YOUR MOJO BACK REVISED. BY AUTHOR ANTHONY POLANCO - MUSIC ARTIST.

FOUNDER OF GODXP. A PERSONAL DEVELOPMENT COMPANY. DIGITAL MARKETING

CONSULTANT. FORMER CHRISTIAN MISSIONARY. AND BRAZILIAN JIU-JITSU COMPETITOR.

FIND MUSIC. WORKSHOPS. + MORE CONTENT LIKE THIS AT GODXP.COM

GODXP PUBLISHING

WATCH VIDEOS + FREE DOWNLOADS + MORE AT
GETYOURMOJOBACKBOOK.COM

- ANTHONYPOLANCO
- GETYOURMOJOBACKBOOK
- MOJOBOOK
- GETYOURMOJOBACKBOOK